AN INVISIBLE MATTER

(A dark matter and black hole of star)

MYSELF

I am here bringing more infermation about stellar evolution black holes and dark matter in the universe. This topic is very curious among students and youngsters and brought from different sources . I brought this book in three different parts. PART-A is the formation of galaxies after the Big Bang. PART-B gives in depth knowledge on stars and black holes. And then PART-C gives basic concepts of dark matter in the universe. Bye D.Suresh

INTRODUCTION

Stellar evolution is the natural process through which stars undergo changes over time, from their formation to their eventual demise. It's a fascinating journey that spans billions of years and involves complex interactions between the forces of gravity, nuclear fusion, and radiation pressure.

Stars are born within vast clouds of gas and dust called nebulae. As these clouds collapse under their own gravity, they heat up and eventually form protostars. Within the core of a protostar, temperatures and pressures continue to rise until nuclear fusion ignites, primarily converting hydrogen into helium. This marks the birth of a true star, as it enters the main sequence phase, where it will spend the majority of its lifetime.

During the main sequence phase, stars like our Sun maintain a delicate balance between the inward pull of gravity and the outward pressure generated by nuclear fusion in their cores. This equilibrium sustains the star's energy output, providing the heat and light that enable life to thrive on planets like Earth.

As stars age and consume their nuclear fuel, their cores begin to contract and heat up, causing the outer layers to expand and cool. This marks the transition into the red giant or supergiant phase, depending on the mass of the star. During this phase, heavier elements produced by nuclear fusion in the core are pushed to the surface, enriching the surrounding space with elements crucial for the formation of new stars and planets.

For stars with lower mass, such as our Sun, the red giant phase culminates in the shedding of its outer layers, forming a planetary nebula, while the core contracts to form a dense, Earth-sized remnant known as a white dwarf. On the other hand, more massive stars undergo dramatic supernova explosions, scattering heavy elements across the cosmos and leaving behind exotic remnants such as neutron stars or black holes.

The study of stellar evolution not only sheds light on the life cycles of individual stars but also plays a crucial role in our understanding of the formation and evolution of galaxies, the synthesis of chemical elements, and the origins of life itself.

INDEX

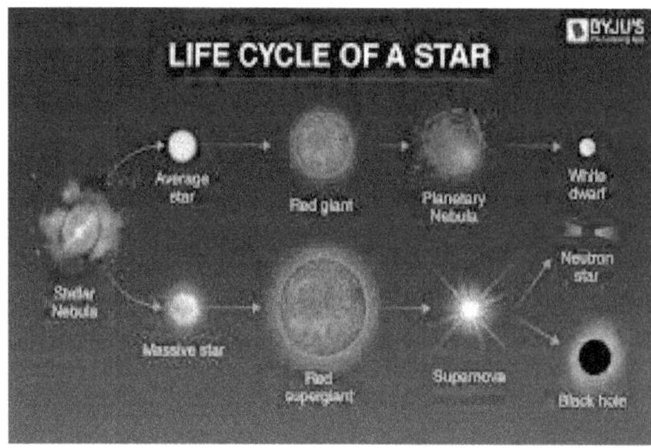

(Taken from BYJUS)

PART-A
BIG BANG

The Big Bang theory is the prevailing cosmological model for the observable universe's earliest known periods. It suggests that the universe began as a hot, dense singularity about 13.8 billion years ago and has been expanding ever since. However, it's not accurately described as an "explosion" in the conventional sense.

Here's a breakdown of the key points:

1. Singularity: The Big Bang theory posits that the universe originated from an extremely hot and dense point, called a singularity. At this point, all matter and energy were concentrated into an infinitely small space.

2. Expansion: Around 13.8 billion years ago, this singularity began to expand rapidly. The universe has been expanding ever since, carrying galaxies away from each other.

3. Formation of Matter: As the universe expanded and cooled down, subatomic particles began to form, eventually leading to

the creation of atoms. These atoms eventually coalesced into clouds, which later formed stars and galaxies.

4. Cosmic Microwave Background (CMB): As the universe expanded and cooled further, about 380,000 years after the initial expansion, protons and electrons combined to form hydrogen atoms. This allowed photons to travel freely, resulting in the release of the cosmic microwave background radiation, which can still be detected today.

5. Galaxy Formation: Over billions of years, gravity caused matter to clump together, forming galaxies, stars, and other cosmic structures.

6. Expansion Continues: The expansion of the universe continues to this day, though the rate of expansion may be accelerating due to dark energy, a mysterious force that counteracts gravity on large scales.

It's crucial to understand that the term "Big Bang" is somewhat misleading, as it wasn't an explosion like one might imagine with an explosion on Earth. Instead, it was the rapid expansion of space itself, along with the subsequent cooling and formation of matter and energy. The Big Bang theory is supported by a wealth of observational evidence, including the cosmic microwave background radiation, the abundance of light elements, and the distribution of galaxies in the universe.

First seconds
After three minutes
After 300,000 years
After 1 billion years
Big bang
After 14 billion years

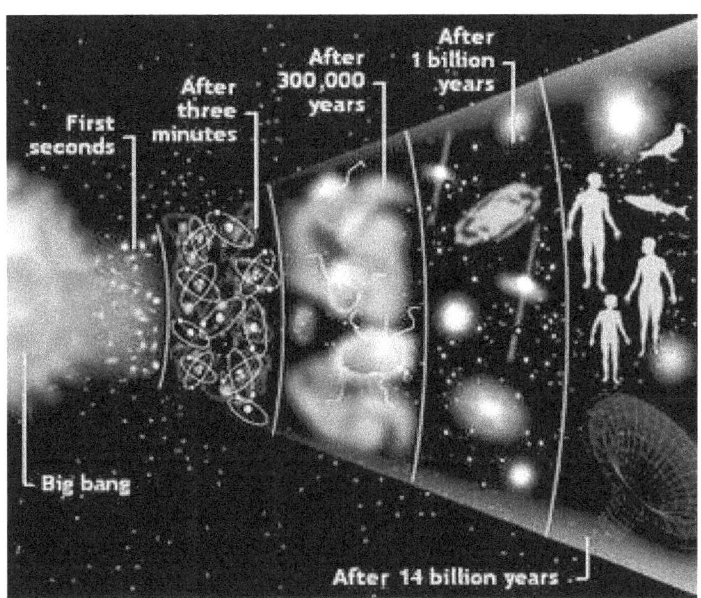

Source

Types of Galaxies
Barred Spiral
Irregular
Spiral
Peculiar
Elliptical
Lenticular

source

FORMATION OF GALAXY

Galaxy formation is a complex process that occurs over billions of years within the framework of cosmology, the study of the origin and evolution of the universe. Here's a simplified overview of how galaxies, such as our own Milky Way, are thought to form:

1. Initial Conditions: Galaxy formation begins with the fluctuations in the density of matter in the early universe. Tiny quantum fluctuations in the density of matter and energy left over from the Big Bang provided the seeds for the formation of structures like galaxies.

2. Dark Matter Halo Formation: Dark matter, a mysterious substance that doesn't emit, absorb, or reflect light and interacts with normal matter only through gravity, plays a crucial role. Dark matter begins to clump together due to gravitational attraction, forming massive structures called dark matter halos. These halos serve as the scaffolding around which galaxies will eventually form.

3. Baryonic Matter Accumulation: Baryonic matter, the ordinary matter we are familiar with (atoms, ions, etc.), is also attracted to the gravitational potential wells created by the dark matter. Over time, gas and dust accumulate within these dark matter halos.

4. Collapse and Star Formation: As the gas and dust accumulate, they become denser and hotter. Eventually, some regions within the clouds of gas and dust become dense enough to collapse under their own gravity. This collapse leads to the formation of stars. These stars, along with gas and dust, are the building blocks of galaxies.

5. Galaxy Growth and Evolution: As more stars form, galaxies grow in size and complexity. Galaxies can undergo mergers with other galaxies, interactions that trigger bursts of star formation, or interactions with the intergalactic medium that affect their evolution.

6. Feedback Processes: Throughout this process, various feedback mechanisms influence the evolution of galaxies. For example, supernova explosions from dying stars can eject gas and dust into the interstellar medium, affecting future star formation. Active galactic nuclei (AGN), powered by supermassive black holes at the centers of galaxies, can also influence the surrounding gas and stars.

7. Galaxy Types and Structures: The characteristics of a galaxy, such as its shape, size, and content, are influenced by its formation history and environment. Galaxies come in various shapes and sizes, including spiral, elliptical, and irregular. These different types reflect the diverse evolutionary paths galaxies can take.

Galaxy formation is an active area of research in astrophysics, and astronomers use observations from telescopes and computer simulations to better understand the processes involved in the formation and evolution of galaxies across cosmic time.

TYPES OF GALAXIES

Galaxies come in various shapes and sizes, and astronomers have classified them into several main types based on their visual appearance. The most common types of galaxies are:

1. Spiral Galaxies: These galaxies have a distinct spiral structure characterized by sweeping arms of stars, dust, and gas rotating around a central bulge. Spiral galaxies often have prominent features like star-forming regions, and they typically contain a significant amount of interstellar matter. Examples include the Milky Way, the Andromeda Galaxy (M31), and the Whirlpool Galaxy (M51).

2. Elliptical Galaxies: Elliptical galaxies are smooth and ellipsoidal in shape, with little or no obvious structure. They often contain older stars and have less interstellar matter compared to spiral galaxies. Elliptical galaxies range from nearly spherical to highly elongated shapes. Examples include M87 in the Virgo Cluster and the massive galaxy Centaurus A.

3. Irregular Galaxies: Irregular galaxies lack a defined shape and structure. They often have irregular shapes, clumpy distributions of stars and gas, and may show evidence of recent interactions or mergers with other galaxies. Irregular galaxies can contain regions of active star formation. Examples include

the Large and Small Magellanic Clouds, which are satellite galaxies of the Milky Way.

4. Lenticular Galaxies: Lenticular galaxies have features of both spiral and elliptical galaxies. They have a disk-like structure similar to spiral galaxies but lack the prominent spiral arms. Lenticular galaxies typically contain older stars and have little ongoing star formation. Examples include the Sombrero Galaxy (M104) and NGC 2787.

5. Dwarf Galaxies: Dwarf galaxies are smaller and less massive than their larger counterparts and are often found orbiting larger galaxies like the Milky Way and Andromeda. They can be elliptical, irregular, or even have some spiral structure. Dwarf galaxies are essential for understanding galaxy formation and evolution. Examples include the Fornax Dwarf Galaxy and the Sculptor Dwarf Galaxy.

These categories provide a basic framework for classifying galaxies, but within each type, there is considerable diversity in terms of size, mass, stellar content, and other properties. Additionally, some galaxies exhibit hybrid characteristics or are undergoing transformations due to interactions with other galaxies or environmental influences.

PART-B

CHAPTER-1

GIANT GAS CLOUD

Stars begin their life as a giant cloud of gas and dust, known as a nebula. The Orion Nebula is an example of a star-forming region.
A gas cloud, commonly known as a nebula, is an immense cloud of dust and gas located in space. Nebulae play a crucial role in the cosmos as they are the birthplaces of stars and planetary systems. Here's a detailed explanation of what a nebula is and its significance:

1. Composition: Nebulae are primarily made up of hydrogen and helium gas, along with dust and other trace elements. These components are the basic building blocks for star formation.
The minimum mass required for a nebula to form a star is determined by the conditions necessary for nuclear fusion to begin in the core of the protostar that will form from the nebula. This is known as the Jeans Mass, and it varies depending on the temperature and density of the nebula, as well as the pressure from the surrounding environment.

For a typical nebula made primarily of hydrogen, the theoretical minimum mass needed to sustain hydrogen fusion and form a main-sequence star is about 0.08 solar masses. This is the threshold at which a protostar can become a red dwarf, the smallest type of main-sequence star. Objects below this mass are known as brown dwarfs and do not have enough mass to sustain hydrogen fusion.

It's important to note that these values are averages and can vary. The actual process of star formation is complex and influenced by many factors, including the nebula's composition and the presence of external forces such as nearby stars or galactic events. However, the 0.08 solar mass figure provides a general guideline for the minimum size of a nebula required to form a star that can sustain nuclear fusion in its core.

2. Formation: Some nebulae form from the remnants of a supernova, which is the explosive death of a star, while others are simply regions where new stars are beginning to form[1].

3. Star Nurseries: Nebulae are often referred to as "star nurseries" because they contain the dense clumps of gas and dust that eventually collapse under their own gravity to form stars.

4. Variety: There are various types of nebulae, including emission nebulae, which glow due to the energy from nearby stars, and reflection nebulae, which shine by reflecting the light of stars.

5. Size: Nebulae can be vast, with some spanning hundreds of light-years across. Despite their size, they are often less dense than any vacuum created on Earth.

6. Observation: Nebulae are observed using powerful telescopes. Space telescopes like NASA's Hubble Space Telescope have captured stunning images of these cosmic phenomena.

7. Examples: The Orion Nebula and the Eagle Nebula's "Pillars of Creation" are famous examples of star-forming regions within nebulae.

Nebulae are not only essential for the creation of new stars but also contribute to the recycling of cosmic material, influencing the evolution of galaxies. They are truly fascinating structures that highlight the ongoing processes of birth and death in the universe.

SOURCE

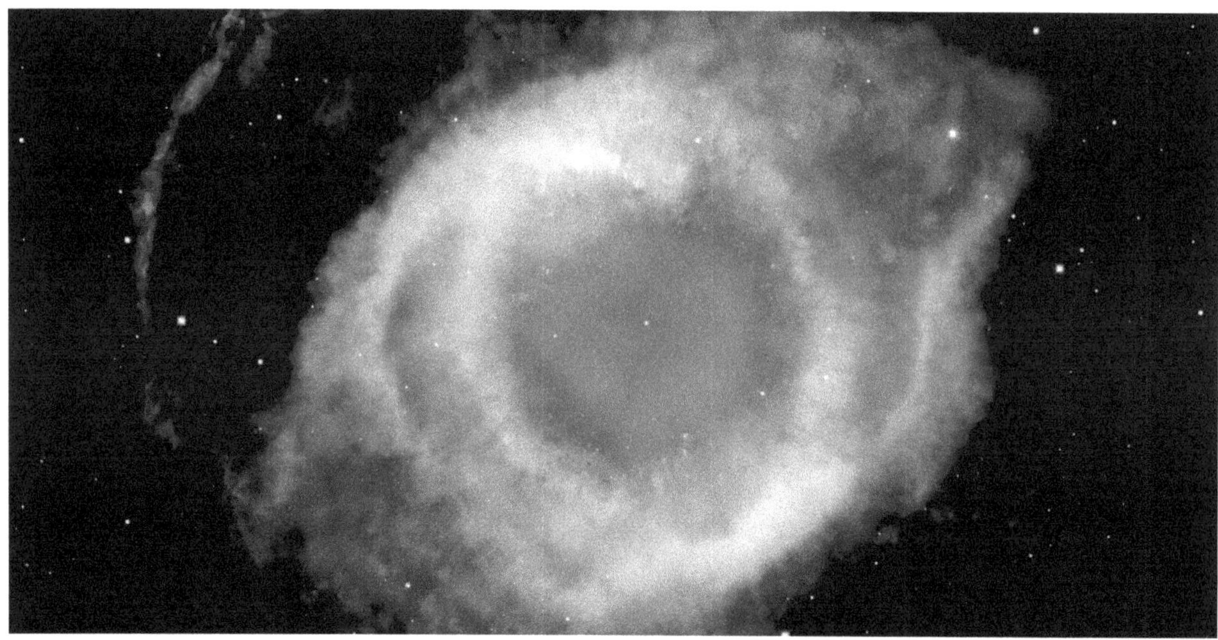

SOURCE

PROTOSTAR(SOURCE)

CHAPTER-2

PROTOSTAR

As the gas and dust in the nebula start to collapse under gravity, they heat up and form a protostar. This is the early stage of a star's formation.

A protostar is a very young star that is in the earliest stage of stellar evolution. It forms when a dense region within a molecular cloud collapses under its own gravity. Here's a detailed look at the protostar stage:

1. Formation: A protostar begins as a dense core within a molecular cloud, which collapses due to gravitational forces. As the core collapses, it heats up and gathers more mass from the surrounding cloud.

2. Accretion: During this stage, the protostar continues to accumulate mass from the parent molecular cloud. This process is known as accretion.

3. Temperature and Luminosity: Although a protostar looks like a star, its core is not yet hot enough for nuclear fusion to occur. The luminosity of a protostar comes from the gravitational energy released as the protostar contracts.

4. Protostellar Disk: As the protostar forms, it is often surrounded by a rotating disk of gas and dust. This disk can eventually form planets and other solar system bodies.

5. Jets and Winds: Many protostars eject material in the form of jets and winds, which can help clear away surrounding material and reveal the protostar.

6. Duration: For a low-mass star, like our Sun, the protostar phase lasts about 500,000 years. The duration of this phase can vary depending on the mass of the protostar.

7. Transition to Main Sequence: A protostar becomes a main-sequence star once its core temperature exceeds 10 million Kelvin, which is the temperature required for hydrogen fusion to begin efficiently.

The protostar phase is a critical period in the life of a star, where it transitions from a cold clump of gas and dust to a hot, shining star. It's a phase full of dynamic changes and sets the stage for the long, stable period of a star's life on the main sequence..

SUPERNOVA EXPLOSION (source)

SUPERNOVA EXPLOSION (source)

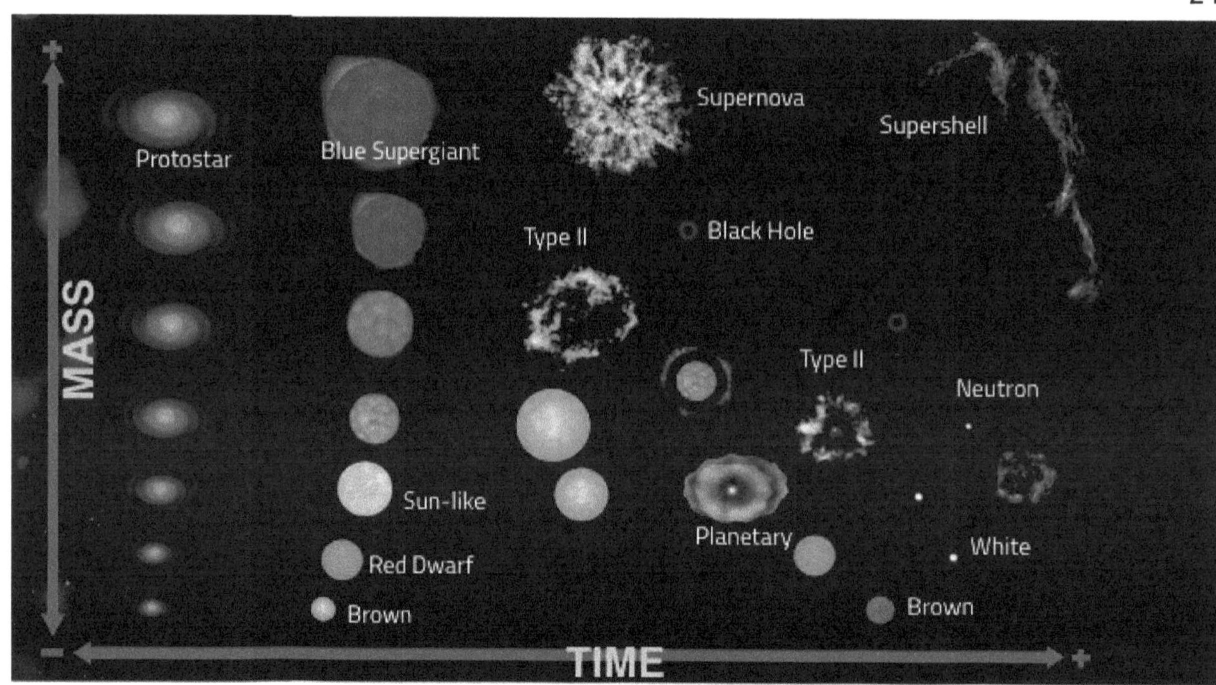

STELLAR EVOLUTION (Source: Chandra X-ray Observatory)

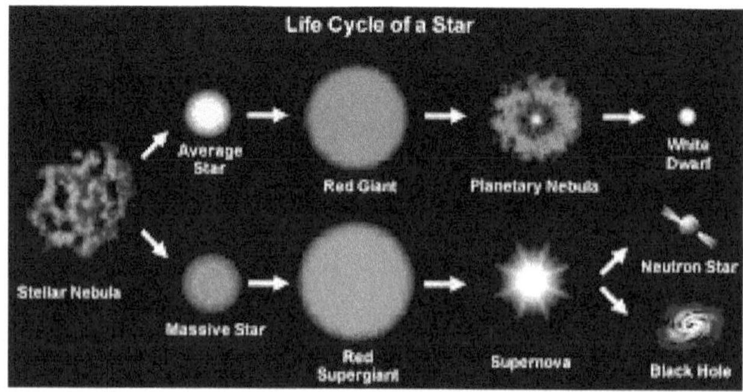

STELLAR EVOLUTION (Source: Scioly.org)

CHAPTER-3

T-TAURI PHASE

After the protostar has formed, it enters the T-Tauri phase. During this time, the star has not yet started nuclear fusion in its core. This phase lasts for about 100 million years.

The T-Tauri phase is a very important stage in the life of a star. It occurs after the protostar stage, when the star is still forming and has not yet begun nuclear fusion in its core. Here's a detailed explanation of the T-Tauri phase:

1. Pre-Main Sequence Stars: T-Tauri stars are pre-main-sequence stars, meaning they are in the process of contracting towards the main sequence, where they will spend most of their lives.

2. Named After T Tauri: This class of stars is named after the prototype star T Tauri, located in the Taurus star-forming region.

3. Characteristics: T-Tauri stars are characterized by their optical variability and strong chromospheric lines. They are less than about ten million years old and are found in molecular clouds.

4. Energy Source: Unlike main-sequence stars, T-Tauri stars do not generate energy through nuclear fusion. Instead, they shine due to gravitational energy released as they contract.

5. Hayashi Track: These stars contract along the Hayashi track, which is a luminosity-temperature relationship followed by infant stars of less than 3 solar masses in the pre-main-sequence phase of stellar evolution.

6. Rotation and Activity: T-Tauri stars typically rotate rapidly, with periods between one and twelve days. They are very active and variable, with intense and variable X-ray and radio emissions.

7. Stellar Winds and Jets: Many T-Tauri stars have powerful stellar winds, and some eject gas in high-velocity bipolar jets. This activity can influence the star's surroundings and contribute to the clearing of material in the vicinity.

8. Circumstellar Disks: These stars often have circumstellar disks, which may contain clumps of material that could eventually form planets and other solar system bodies.

9. Lithium Abundance: The spectra of T-Tauri stars show a higher lithium abundance than main-sequence stars because lithium is destroyed at higher temperatures. This abundance provides clues about the star's age and evolutionary stage.

The T-Tauri phase ends when a star develops a radiative zone, or when a smaller star begins nuclear fusion on the main sequence. This phase is crucial for the star's development and can last up to 100 million years for stars with less than 3 solar masses. It's a dynamic period filled with changes that will determine the future characteristics and lifespan of the star.

CHAPTER-4

MAIN SEQUENCE OF EVOLUTION

This is the longest stage of a star's life. Nuclear fusion begins, converting hydrogen into helium and releasing energy. Our Sun is currently in this phase.

The main sequence is a critical phase in the life of a star, representing a period of relative stability in its lifecycle. Here's an explanation of the main sequence:

1. Hydrogen Fusion: Main sequence stars fuse hydrogen atoms to form helium atoms in their cores. This nuclear fusion releases a tremendous amount of energy, which provides the light and heat we receive from stars like our Sun.

2. Stellar Equilibrium: During the main sequence phase, a star is in hydrostatic equilibrium. The outward pressure from the energy produced by nuclear fusion balances the inward gravitational forces trying to collapse the star.

3. Lifespan: The time a star spends on the main sequence depends on its mass. Larger, more massive stars burn through their hydrogen fuel more quickly and have shorter main sequence lifespans. For example, while the Sun is expected to remain on the main sequence for about 10 billion years, a star 10 times as massive might only stay in this phase for 20 million years.

4. Variability: Main sequence stars can vary greatly in size, luminosity, and color. They range from small, cool red dwarfs to massive, hot blue giants.

5. End of the Main Sequence: A star remains on the main sequence as long as it has hydrogen to fuse in its core. When the hydrogen is depleted, the star leaves the main sequence and enters the next phase of its evolution, which for a star like the Sun, would be the red giant phase.

6. Significance: About 90% of the stars in the universe are in the main sequence phase at any given time, including our Sun. This phase is significant because it's during the main sequence that stars are stable and emit consistent energy, making conditions possible for life on planets like Earth.

The main sequence is not only the most prolonged stage in a star's life but also the most productive, as it's during this time that stars contribute most to the energy output of galaxies..

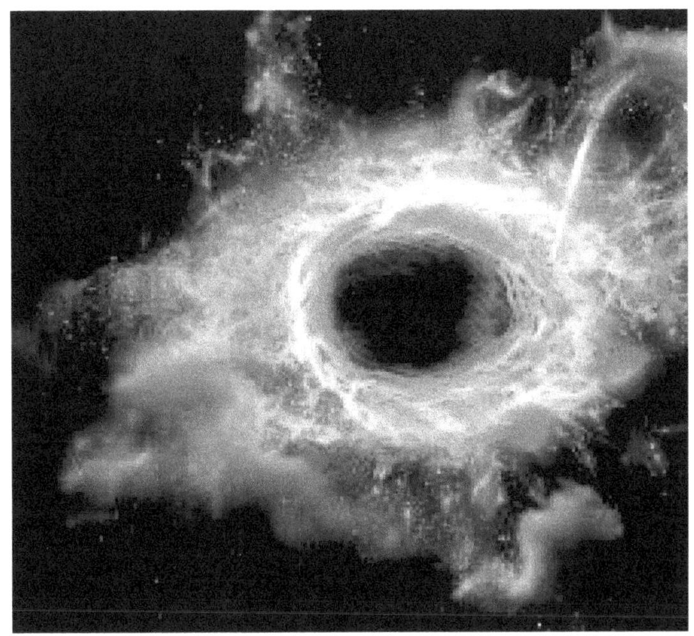

SOURCE

CHAPTER-5

RED GIANT

Once the hydrogen in the core is exhausted, the star expands and cools to become a red giant. For medium-sized stars like the Sun, this is the next stage after the main sequence.

A red giant is a stage in the life cycle of a star that occurs after it has exhausted the supply of hydrogen in its core for nuclear fusion. Here's a detailed explanation of a red giant:

1. Core Hydrogen Exhaustion: When a star uses up the hydrogen in its core, the core contracts and heats up. This increased temperature ignites hydrogen fusion in a shell surrounding the inert helium core.

2. Expansion and Cooling: As the core contracts, the outer layers of the star expand and cool, causing the star to grow in size and its surface temperature to decrease. This gives the star a reddish hue, hence the name "red giant".

3. Luminosity: Despite the cooler surface temperature, red giants are very luminous due to their large size. They can be tens to hundreds of times more luminous than the Sun.

4. Surface Temperature: The surface temperature of a red giant is around 5,000 K (4,700 °C; 8,500 °F) or lower, which is cooler than the Sun's surface temperature.

5. Spectral Types: Red giants have spectral types of K or M, and sometimes G. They may also include class S stars and most carbon stars.

6. End of Life: Eventually, a red giant will shed its outer layers, often creating a planetary nebula. The core that remains will become a white dwarf.

7. The Sun's Future: Our own Sun will eventually become a red giant in about five billion years. As it expands, it is expected to engulf the inner planets, including Earth.

Red giants represent a late phase of stellar evolution for stars of low or intermediate mass (roughly 0.3–8 solar masses). They are fascinating objects because they mark a transition between the stable main sequence phase and the final stages of a star's life..

CHAPTER-6.

FUSION OF HEAVIER ELEMENTS

In more massive stars, the core contracts and heats up further, allowing fusion of heavier elements like carbon and oxygen.

The fusion of heavier elements in stars is a complex process that occurs after a star has exhausted its hydrogen fuel. This process, known as stellar nucleosynthesis, involves the fusion of lighter elements into heavier ones and is responsible for creating many of the elements found in the universe. Here's an overview of how this process works:

1. Helium Fusion: Once the hydrogen in a star's core is depleted, the core contracts and heats up, allowing helium to fuse into carbon and oxygen. This is known as the triple-alpha process.

2. Carbon Burning: As the core temperature increases, carbon atoms can fuse together to form heavier elements like neon and magnesium.

3. Neon Burning: At even higher temperatures, neon can undergo fusion to produce oxygen and magnesium.

4. Oxygen Burning: Oxygen atoms can fuse to create silicon and sulfur. This stage requires extremely high temperatures and pressures.

5. Silicon Burning: The fusion of silicon is the last stage of nuclear burning for a star. Silicon burns to produce a range of elements up to iron.

6. Iron Core: Iron cannot release energy by fusion because it has the highest binding energy per nucleon of all the elements. When a star's core is converted to iron, it no longer generates pressure to support the outer layers against gravity.

7. Supernova Nucleosynthesis: For massive stars, the end result is a supernova explosion, which can produce elements heavier than iron through processes like neutron capture (the r-process and s-process), proton capture (the rp-process), and photodisintegration (the p-process).

The fusion of heavier elements occurs in the most massive stars and is a critical part of the cycle of matter in the universe. It's through these processes that stars contribute to the cosmic abundance of elements, enriching the interstellar medium with the materials necessary for forming new stars, planets, and ultimately, life itself.

CHAPTER-7

SUPERNOVA EXPLOSION

Depending on the mass, a star will end its life in a dramatic supernova explosion or a more gentle ejection of its outer layers as a planetary nebula. The core that remains can become a neutron star or black hole (for massive stars) or a white dwarf (for stars like the Sun).

A supernova explosion is one of the most powerful and luminous events in the universe, marking the death of a star. Here's an explanation of what happens during a supernova:

1. End of Stellar Life: A supernova occurs during the last evolutionary stages of a massive star or when a white dwarf is triggered into runaway nuclear fusion.

2. Massive Star Supernova: For a massive star, a supernova happens when the star runs out of nuclear fuel and its core collapses under the force of gravity. The core heats up and eventually reaches a point where it can no longer support the layers above it, leading to a catastrophic collapse.

3. White Dwarf Supernova: In a binary star system, a white dwarf may accumulate enough matter from its companion star, or merge with another white dwarf, to reach a critical mass and trigger a thermonuclear explosion.

4. Explosion Mechanics: The collapse of a massive star's core or the ignition of a white dwarf leads to an enormous shock wave that blasts the star's outer layers into space at speeds of thousands of kilometers per second.

5. Luminosity: Supernovae can briefly outshine entire galaxies and can be seen across vast intergalactic distances. They are bright enough to be observable from Earth even if they occur in distant galaxies.

6. Nucleosynthesis: Supernovae are responsible for creating many of the heavy elements in the universe, such as iron, which are then dispersed into the interstellar medium.

7. Remnants: The aftermath of a supernova can leave behind a neutron star or black hole if the original star was sufficiently massive. Otherwise, it may leave a diffuse nebula.

8. Cosmic Importance: Supernovae play a crucial role in the cosmos. They distribute heavy elements necessary for new stars and planets, influence the formation of new stars, and contribute to the chemical complexity of the universe.

Supernovae are not only spectacular to observe but also fundamental to our understanding of the universe, including the origin of elements and the expansion of space. They are rare events, with only a few occurring per century in a galaxy like the Milky Way. The last supernova observed with the naked eye in our galaxy was Kepler's Supernova in 1604..

CHAPTER-8

PLANETARY NEBULA

A planetary nebula is a fascinating astronomical phenomenon that represents the end of life for medium-sized stars. Here's a detailed explanation:

1. Formation: A planetary nebula forms when a star like our Sun, at the end of its life, expels its outer layers into space. This occurs after the red giant phase, when the star has used up its nuclear fuel.

2. Central Star: The core that remains after the outer layers are ejected becomes a hot, dense stellar remnant known as a white dwarf. This white dwarf emits intense ultraviolet radiation.

3. Ionized Gas Shell: The expelled outer layers form a shell of ionized gas around the white dwarf. The ultraviolet radiation from the central star ionizes the gas, causing it to glow and form the nebula.

4. Misnomer: The term "planetary nebula" is actually a misnomer. Early astronomers named them so because they appeared planet-like in their telescopes, but they have nothing to do with planets.

5. Life Span: Planetary nebulae are relatively short-lived on a cosmic scale, lasting only a few tens of thousands of years before dissipating into the surrounding interstellar medium.

6. Chemical Enrichment: They play a crucial role in the chemical evolution of galaxies by dispersing elements like carbon and nitrogen, which were formed in the star, into space.

7. Observation: Many planetary nebulae have been observed, and they exhibit a variety of shapes and sizes. Some are spherical, while others have more complex structures.

8. Examples: Famous examples include the Ring Nebula and the Helix Nebula, which showcase the beauty and complexity of these cosmic objects.

In essence, planetary nebulae are the beautiful, glowing remnants of stars that have finished their nuclear burning stages. They contribute to the cycle of stellar evolution by returning material to the interstellar medium, where it can eventually form new stars and planets..

NEUTRON STAR

After a heavy star undergoes a supernova explosion, the subsequent stages depend on the mass of the remnant core. Here's what happens to the core of a heavy star post-supernova:

1. Neutron Star: If the core remnant is between about 1.4 and 3 times the mass of our Sun, it will become a neutron star. Neutron stars are incredibly dense, with the mass of a Sun compressed into a city-sized sphere.

2. Black Hole: If the core remnant is more than roughly 3 times the mass of our Sun, it will collapse further to become a black hole. A black hole has such strong gravity that not even light can escape from it.

3. Pulsar: Some neutron stars can become pulsars. Pulsars are rapidly rotating neutron stars that emit beams of electromagnetic radiation out of their magnetic poles. If these beams sweep across Earth, they can be detected as pulses of radiation.

4. Magnetar: A subset of neutron stars with extremely powerful magnetic fields are known as magnetars. These objects can emit intense bursts of X-rays and gamma rays.

5. Supernova Remnant: The material ejected during the supernova explosion forms a supernova remnant. This expanding shell of gas and dust can be observed for thousands of years as it interacts with the surrounding interstellar medium.

6. Nucleosynthesis: The supernova event is also responsible for the creation of heavy elements through a process called supernova nucleosynthesis. Elements heavier than iron are formed during the explosion and dispersed into space.

These remnants and processes play a crucial role in the evolution of galaxies, contributing to the cosmic cycle of matter and the formation of new stars and planetary systems. The exact path of evolution for a heavy star's core after a supernova explosion is determined by the laws of physics and the initial mass of the star.

A neutron star is the incredibly dense remnant of a massive supergiant star that has ended its life in a supernova explosion. Here's a detailed explanation of a neutron star:

1. Formation: Neutron stars form from the collapsed core of a massive star after a supernova explosion. The core's collapse compresses it to an extremely high density, surpassing even that of a white dwarf.

2. Size and Mass: Neutron stars are incredibly small compared to their mass. They typically have a radius of about 10 kilometers (6 miles) but can have a mass up to 1.4 times that of our Sun.

3. Density: They are among the densest objects in the universe, with densities comparable to that of atomic nuclei. A matchbox-sized amount of neutron star material would weigh approximately 3 billion tonnes.

4. Composition: Most models suggest neutron stars are composed almost entirely of neutrons, created by the pressure-induced fusion of electrons and protons present in normal matter.

5. Degeneracy Pressure: Neutron stars are supported against further collapse by neutron degeneracy pressure, similar to how electron degeneracy pressure supports white dwarfs.

6. Temperature: Newly formed neutron stars can have surface temperatures of ten million Kelvin or more. Over time, they cool down, as they do not generate new heat through fusion.

7. Magnetic Fields: Neutron stars have extremely strong magnetic fields, which can be billions of times stronger than Earth's magnetic field. This affects the surface iron, causing it to form long chains of iron atoms.

8. Pulsars: Some neutron stars are observed as pulsars, which are rapidly rotating neutron stars that emit beams of electromagnetic radiation. These beams can be detected as pulses when they sweep past Earth.

9. End of Life: If a neutron star's mass exceeds the Tolman–Oppenheimer–Volkoff limit (around 2.2–2.9 solar masses), it can collapse further to form a black hole.

Neutron stars are fascinating objects that provide insights into the extreme conditions that matter can exist under and the complex life cycles of massive stars. They continue to be a subject of intense study in astrophysics.

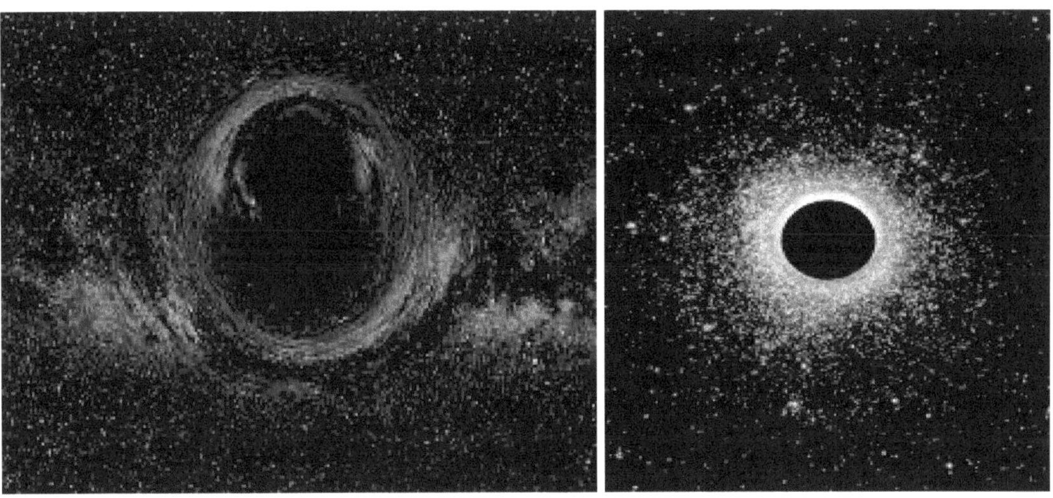

SOURCE

FINAL STAGES OF A BLACK HOLE

A heavy black hole, often referred to as a supermassive black hole, is a type of black hole that has a mass millions to billions of times greater than that of our Sun. Here's an explanation of how these heavy black holes are related to stars:

1. Stellar Black Holes: Black holes of stellar mass form when massive stars collapse at the end of their life cycle. After a supernova explosion, if the remaining core's mass is sufficient, it collapses into a black hole.

2. Growth: Once formed, black holes can grow by absorbing mass from their surroundings. This includes gas, dust, and other stellar material.

3. Supermassive Black Holes: Supermassive black holes, which are found at the centers of most galaxies, including our Milky Way, may form by absorbing other stars and merging with other black holes. They can also form from the direct collapse of massive gas clouds.

4. Influence on Star Formation: Interestingly, while black holes are often thought of as destructive, they can also play a role in star formation. For instance, the gravitational pull of a supermassive black hole can compress nearby gas and dust, triggering the formation of new stars.

5. Accretion Disks: Material falling into a black hole can form an accretion disk around it. The friction within this disk can heat the material to very high temperatures, causing it to emit intense radiation, including visible light.

6. Quasars and Active Galactic Nuclei: When the accretion disk of a supermassive black hole emits an extraordinary amount of light, the black hole can be observed as a quasar or an active galactic nucleus (AGN), making it one of the brightest objects in the universe.

7. Galactic Dynamics: Supermassive black holes have a significant impact on the dynamics of their host galaxies. They can influence the motion of stars and gas and play a role in the evolution of the galaxy.

8. Event Horizon: The boundary around a black hole from which nothing can escape, not even light, is called the event horizon. This is the point of no return for matter falling into the black hole.

9. Hawking Radiation: According to quantum field theory, black holes can emit radiation, known as Hawking radiation. This radiation is due to quantum effects near the event horizon.

DURING SUPERNOVA EXPLOSION

Supermassive black holes are still a subject of intense study and debate among astronomers. They are fundamental to our understanding of the universe's structure and the life cycle of galaxies. The exact processes by which they form and influence their surroundings continue to be key questions in astrophysics.

Black holes, as we understand them, do not explode in the traditional sense. They are regions of space where gravity is so strong that nothing, not even light, can escape from them. However, there are a few scenarios in which a black hole can be involved in an explosive event or release significant amounts of energy:

1. Hawking Radiation: According to theoretical physicist Stephen Hawking, black holes can emit radiation due to quantum effects near their event horizon. This radiation, known as Hawking radiation, causes the black hole to lose mass over time. For a black hole of stellar mass, this process is extremely slow. However, for very small black holes, this radiation could cause them to lose mass more rapidly and eventually lead to an explosive release of energy as they evaporate.

2. Supernova Explosion: While a black hole itself doesn't explode, it can be the result of a supernova explosion, which is the catastrophic death of a massive star. After the star's core collapses under its own gravity, the outer layers can be expelled

in a massive explosion, leaving behind a black hole if the core's mass is sufficient.

3. Tidal Disruption Events: If a star passes too close to a black hole, it can be torn apart by the black hole's tidal forces in a tidal disruption event. The in-falling material can form an accretion disk around the black hole and release a tremendous amount of energy, sometimes observed as a bright flare.

4. Black Hole Mergers: When two black holes merge, they can release a significant amount of energy in the form of gravitational waves. These events are not explosions in the traditional sense but are among the most powerful events in the universe.

5. Relativistic Jets: Some black holes, particularly supermassive black holes at the centers of galaxies, can emit powerful jets of particles at nearly the speed of light. While these jets are not an explosion of the black hole itself, they can release energy comparable to that of an explosion and can be observed across vast distances.

It's important to note that these processes are different from the kind of explosive events associated with stars, such as novae or supernovae. Black holes are fundamentally different objects, and their interactions with surrounding matter and energy can lead to some of the most extreme phenomena in the universe.

SUPERNOVA EXPLOSION (Source: link)

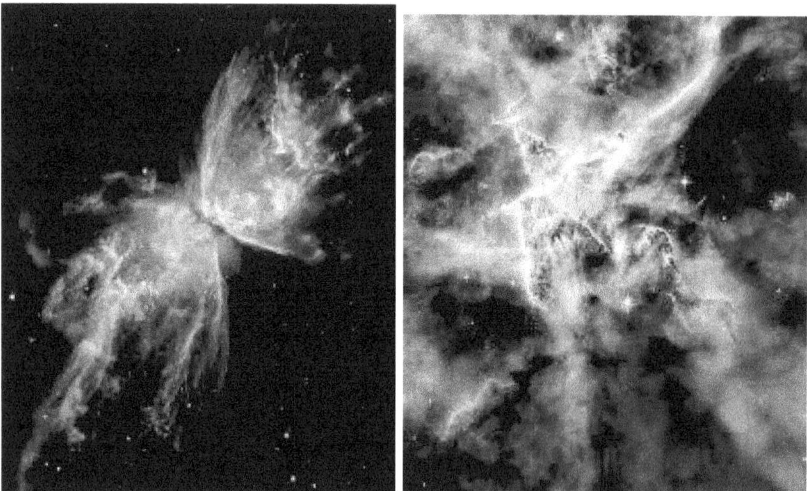

SUPERNOVA EXPLOSION (source link)

COLLAPSING BACK HOLES

When two massive black holes come close enough to affect each other gravitationally, they begin to orbit one another, spiraling inwards due to the emission of gravitational waves. This process is known as inspiral. As they spiral closer and closer, they eventually merge into a single, larger black hole during a highly energetic event. Here's what happens during and after the collision:

1. Inspiraling: The black holes lose energy through the emission of gravitational waves, causing them to move closer together.

2. Merger: When they are sufficiently close, they will merge into a single black hole in a process that releases a significant amount of energy in the form of gravitational waves.

3. Gravitational Waves: These waves are ripples in the fabric of space-time that travel outward from the merger at the speed of light, carrying information about the event.

4. Ringdown: After the merger, the new black hole goes through a phase called ringdown, where it settles into a stable shape (usually a sphere) and emits a final burst of gravitational waves.

5. Kick: In some cases, the newly formed black hole can receive a "kick" from the asymmetric emission of gravitational waves, potentially propelling it out of its host galaxy.

6. Energy Release: The collision of two massive black holes is one of the most powerful events in the universe, with the energy released in gravitational waves being immense.

7. Observation: Events like these can be observed by detectors such as LIGO, Virgo, and KAGRA, which can pick up the gravitational waves produced by such colossal mergers.

The merger of two massive black holes is a cosmic event of great significance, providing insights into the nature of gravity, the behavior of black holes, and the dynamics of galaxies. It's a phenomenon that confirms predictions made by Einstein's theory of general relativity and helps astronomers understand the evolution of the universe.

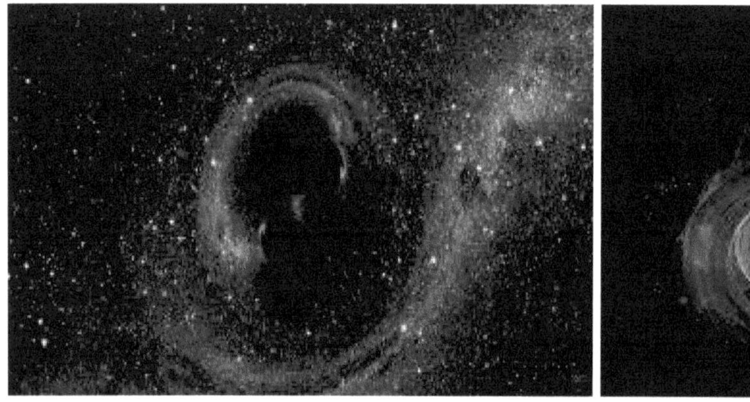

COLLIDING TWO BLACK HOLES (source link))

PART-C

Dark matter is a mysterious and invisible substance that makes up a significant portion of the universe's mass. Here's an explanation of dark matter:

1. Invisible Substance: Dark matter does not emit, absorb, or reflect light, making it invisible to current telescopes. Its presence is inferred from its gravitational effects on visible matter, radiation, and the large-scale structure of the universe.

2. Gravitational Effects: The existence of dark matter was first suggested due to the observation that galaxies were spinning faster than could be accounted for by the visible matter alone. Dark matter provides the additional gravity needed to prevent these galaxies from flying apart.

3. Cosmic Glue: Dark matter acts like a cosmic glue, holding galaxies and galaxy clusters together. Without it, the structure of the universe on large scales would be very different.

4. Dominant Mass Component: It is estimated that dark matter makes up about 27% of the universe, while the familiar "ordinary" matter only makes up less than 5%. The rest is dark energy, which is responsible for the accelerated expansion of the universe.

5. Detection Methods: Although we cannot see dark matter, we can detect its presence through its gravitational influence on the

motion of galaxies and the bending of light (gravitational lensing) from distant objects.

6. Galactic Rotation Curves: The rotation curves of galaxies, which show the speed of stars as they orbit the galaxy's center, do not decrease with distance as expected if only visible matter were present. This discrepancy suggests the presence of dark matter.

7. Cosmological Models: Dark matter is a crucial component in cosmological models, helping to explain the formation and evolution of galaxies and the observed anisotropies in the cosmic microwave background radiation.

8. Nature of Dark Matter: The exact nature of dark matter is still unknown, and it remains one of the greatest mysteries in science. Various candidates have been proposed, including weakly interacting massive particles (WIMPs), axions, and sterile neutrinos.

Understanding dark matter is essential for a complete picture of the universe and the laws that govern it. Despite its elusive nature, ongoing research and new experiments aim to detect dark matter particles directly and uncover their properties.

Black holes and dark matter are distinct concepts in astrophysics. Black holes are regions of space where gravity is so strong that nothing, not even light, can escape. They are formed from the remnants of massive stars or by other means such as the collapse of huge amounts of matter.

Dark matter, on the other hand, is a form of matter that does not emit, absorb, or reflect light, making it invisible. It has not been directly observed, but its existence is inferred from its gravitational effects on visible matter and the structure of the universe. Dark matter is thought to make up about 27% of the universe's mass-energy content.

There are theories that suggest primordial black holes, which could have formed shortly after the Big Bang, might account for some or all of the dark matter in the universe. However, this is still a subject of active research and debate. The majority view in the scientific community is that dark matter consists of some type of elementary particles that have yet to be discovered or understood, rather than being made up of black holes.

In summary, while black holes are well-understood and observed astronomical objects, dark matter remains one of the great mysteries of modern cosmology, and its exact nature and composition are still unknown.

Hubble Spots a Galaxy Hidden in a Dark Cloud

SOURCE

Experimental efforts to detect dark matter directly have been ongoing for several decades, but thus far, no conclusive detection has been made. However, several experiments have provided intriguing results that have narrowed down the possible properties of dark matter and spurred further research. Here are some of the key experimental approaches and findings related to dark matter:

1. Direct Detection Experiments: These experiments aim to detect dark matter particles interacting with ordinary matter directly. They typically use underground detectors shielded from cosmic rays to minimize background noise. One of the most well-known direct detection experiments is the Cryogenic Dark Matter Search (CDMS), which uses semiconductor detectors to search for interactions between dark matter particles and atomic nuclei.

2. XENON Collaboration: The XENON collaboration operates a series of experiments using liquid xenon as a target for dark matter particles. The XENON1T experiment, located underground in Italy, set stringent limits on the interaction cross-sections of dark matter particles with ordinary matter. The

successor experiment, XENONnT, aims to further improve sensitivity.

3. LUX and LZ Experiments: The Large Underground Xenon (LUX) experiment, located in the Sanford Underground Research Facility in South Dakota, and its successor, the LUX-ZEPLIN (LZ) experiment, are also searching for dark matter using liquid xenon detectors. While LUX did not detect dark matter, it placed stringent limits on the possible properties of dark matter particles.

4. Dark Matter Annihilation and Decay: Dark matter particles may annihilate or decay into standard model particles, producing observable signals such as gamma rays, neutrinos, or cosmic rays. Experiments such as the Fermi Gamma-ray Space Telescope and the High Energy Stereoscopic System (HESS) have searched for gamma-ray signatures of dark matter annihilation in regions of high dark matter density, such as the center of our galaxy.

5. Indirect Detection with Cosmic Rays: Cosmic ray experiments, such as the Alpha Magnetic Spectrometer (AMS-02) on the International Space Station, search for excesses of cosmic rays that could be produced by dark matter annihilation or decay in the Milky Way or other galaxies.

6. Collider Experiments: Particle accelerators like the Large Hadron Collider (LHC) at CERN in Geneva, Switzerland, also search for evidence of dark matter through indirect production or interaction with ordinary matter. While no direct detection of

dark matter has been made at colliders, experiments like ATLAS and CMS continue to probe for signs of new particles that could be related to dark matter.

While these experiments have not yet directly detected dark matter, they have placed increasingly stringent limits on the possible properties of dark matter particles, ruling out certain theoretical models and guiding the development of new experimental and theoretical approaches. The search for dark matter continues to be one of the most active areas of research in particle physics and astrophysics.

—-------<<<>>>--------

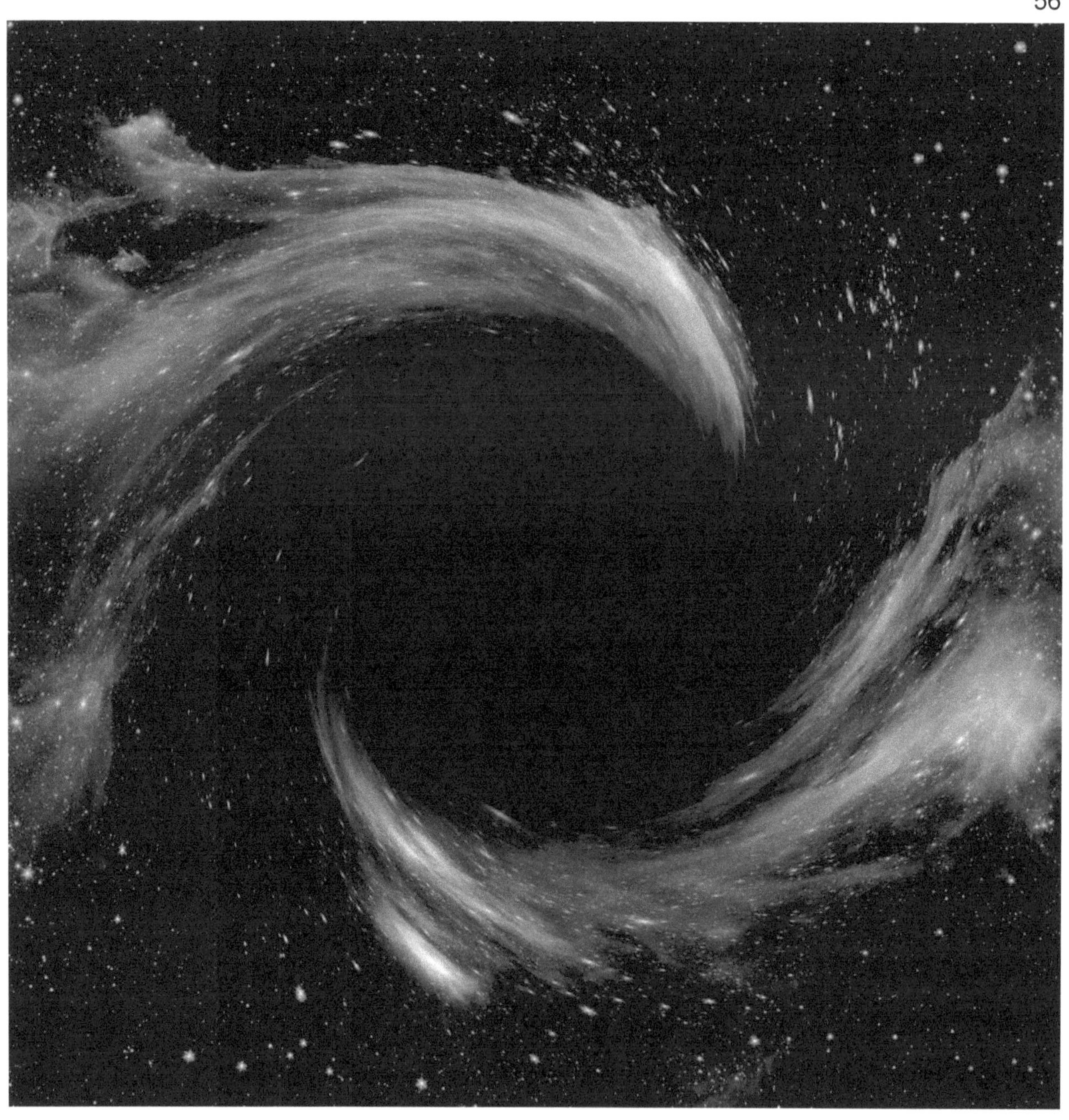

Source

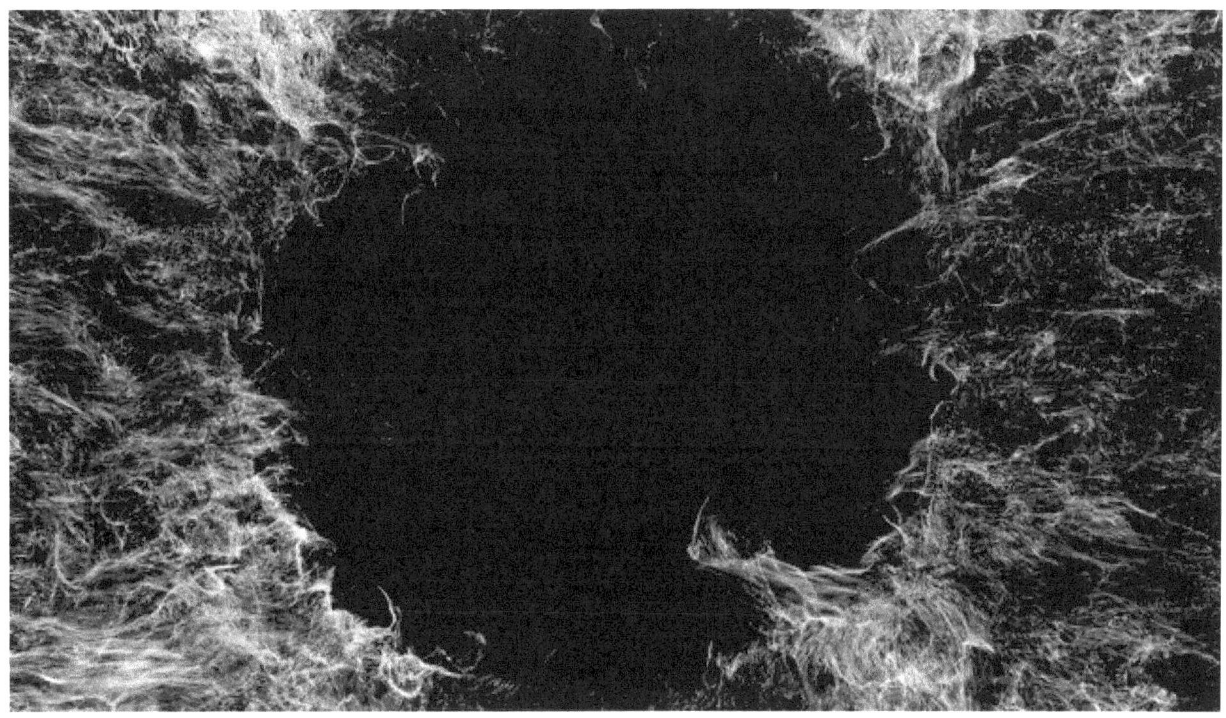

Source

www.ingramcontent.com/pod-product-compliance
Lightning Source LLC
LaVergne TN
LVHW070943160826
845679LV00022B/1898
* 9 7 9 8 8 9 4 4 6 0 0 0 0 *